A GOLDEN SOUVENIR OF
THAILAND

A GOLDEN SOUVENIR OF THAILAND

Photography by Photobank
Text by John Hoskin

ASIA BOOKS

Published and distributed in Thailand by Asia Books Co. Ltd., 5 Soi 61 Sukhumvit Rd., Bangkok, Thailand P.O. Box 40, Bangkok 10110
Tel. (662) 392-0910, 391-2680
Fax (662) 381-1621, 391-2277

Text and captions by John Hoskin

Photography by:
Luca Invernizzi Tettoni, Photobank, with additional photographs from Photobank by Alberto Cassio (8—9, 15 top, 38, 40—41, 66 top/bottom, 67, 68); Michael Freeman (56, 57, 58, 63, 72, 73 top/bottom); Jean Kugler (2—3); Ian Lloyd (35 right, 47); Ben Nakayama (28); Photobank Photo Library (39, 64—65); Duangdao Suwannarangsi (42—43, 54—55 left); Steve Vidler (15 bottom, 33, 53, 69); Bill Wassman (14 top, 55 right). Photograph page 74 by Jacky Yip, China Photo Library.

Designed by Joan Law Design & Photography

Printed in China

ISBN : 962-217-105-2

Title spread
Distinguished by its finger-like towers, Wat Arun, the Temple of the Dawn, is a Bangkok landmark. It was built as the royal chapel of King Taksin (reigned 1767-82) when Thonburi on the west bank of the Chao Phya River was the capital. The central tower is decorated with embedded pieces of multi-coloured porcelain.

Right
The charm and hospitality of people everywhere, however, are as constant as the serene gaze of a Buddha image.

Pages 6-7
Man and buffalo are two quintessentially Thai figures in the landscape. Three-quarters of the population still earns its livelihood from the land. Wet rice cultivation is the mainstay of agriculture and farmers, especially in the semi-arid northeast region, are dependent on the timely arrival of the rains during the June-October monsoon season.

Pages 8-9
The Floating Market at Damnoen Saduak, on the outskirts of Bangkok, presents a scene scarcely changed by the passage of time. The sight of fruit and vegetables being sold from small sampans *plying narrow* klongs *(canals) gives a wonderful insight into traditional waterborne life in Thailand.*

Pages 10-11
Modern Bangkok, a city of nearly six million inhabitants, sprawls across a vast alluvial plain. It has expanded rapidly in recent years, and Silom Road (centre), in the heart of the business district, is flanked by highrise blocks, most of which have sprung up in the 1980s.

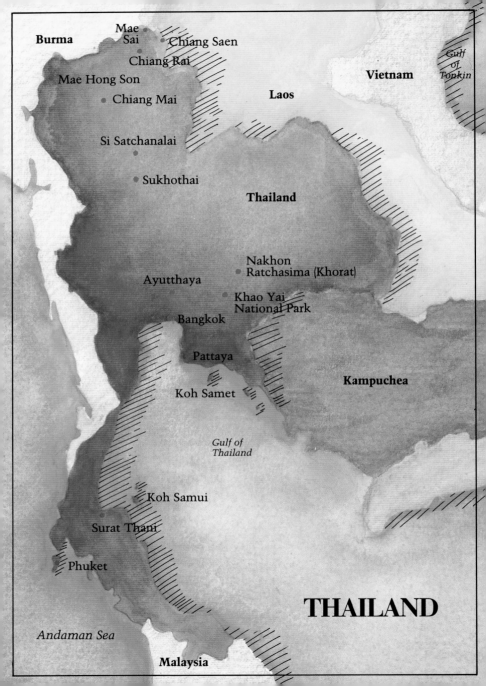

INTRODUCTION

THAILAND IS often dubbed 'the most exotic country in Asia', and with good reason. It offers a distinct culture with a rich and varied heritage, and it possesses a remarkable range of scenic beauty. Yet it is the Thais themselves, with their uncanny ability to blend a respect for the past with a delight in the modern, that makes the country truly intriguing.

Whenever the national airline adds a new aircraft to its fleet, the several million dollars' worth of equipment is blessed by a senior Buddhist monk. Similarly every new office building is inaugurated with propitious rites. In this strange, paradoxical blend of age-old tradition and modern dynamism lies the very essence of Thailand, the uniqueness that sets it apart.

This exotic land, located almost equidistant between India and China, is a tropical country of 514,000 square kilometres (198,400 square miles) — about the same size as France. It is bordered by Burma to the west, Laos to the north, Kampuchea to the east and Malaysia to the south. Distances range from 1,650 kilometres (1,025 miles) north to south and, at the broadest point, 800 kilometres (500 miles) east to west. The narrow Kra peninsula in the south and the shores of the Gulf of Thailand give more than 2,500 kilometres (1,550 miles) of coastline.

The population of 52.8 million (1986 estimate) is now growing at less than two percent, down from more than three percent in the 1960s, following a successful nationwide family-planning campaign. Ethnic Thais form a majority, though the area has historically been a migratory crossroads. Thus strains of Mon, Khmer, Burmese, Lao, Malay, Indian and, most strongly, Chinese stock produce a degree of ethnic diversity. Integration is such, however, that culturally and socially there is enormous unity.

Thailand's focal point is the capital, Bangkok. As the centre of all major political, administrative, commercial, industrial and financial activity it is a modern, sprawling metropolis, its skyline pierced by the thrusting tower blocks of offices, condominiums, luxury hotels and tinselled department stores.

Yet this Western-inspired appearance is largely a facade, and Bangkok does preserve a remarkable amount of its cultural heritage. The soaring roofs and gilded spires of the Grand Palace and the city's many historic temples present a picture of almost fairytale medieval Oriental splendour. And contained within Bangkok's monuments and sights are treasures of the nation's art and cultural endeavour that typify the land and the people. More than anywhere else in the country, Bangkok expresses that essential paradox of adherence to tradition and vibrant involvement with modern development. The successful balancing of tradition and modernity is itself an indication of a national trait.

There is a cohesiveness through continuity, which indelibly stamps the nation and which imparts a quintessential 'Thainess' to it. The word *thai* means 'free' and the nation is the 'land of the free'. This sounds suspiciously trite, and yet the freedom which has permitted historical consistency and the retention of underpinning character traits both defines the country and sustains a pleasing individuality.

Thailand's history as a sovereign state goes back 750 years to the founding of the first capital, Sukhothai, in the early 13th century. This initial power base enjoyed total autonomy for little more than 100 years, but in that time national patterns were forged. The roots of today's political, religious, social and cultural systems can all, to a greater or lesser degree, be traced back to this period.

The second capital, Ayutthaya, founded in 1350, rapidly eclipsed Sukhothai and was the heart of the nation until it was sacked and razed by the Burmese in 1767. Defeat was literally catastrophic but, in a remarkable display of resilience, the Thais quickly reorganized themselves under King Taksin and soon expelled the invaders.

Faces of Thailand. The appearance and costumes of the people differ in various parts of the country, ranging from colourfully attired hilltribes in the North (top) to Muslims in the South (middle) and to typically hard-working farmers in the Northeast (above).

Taksin had set up a new capital on the west bank of the Chao Phya River. It was his successor, King Rama I, founder of the present Chakri dynasty, who established Bangkok as his power base, on the east side of the Chao Phya River about 85 kilometres (53 miles) downsteam from Ayutthaya. Bangkok, known to the Thais as Krung Thep (City of Angels), soon rivalled Ayutthaya in beauty.

Aside from the inevitable vagaries of historical fortune, the development of Thailand — or Siam as it was called until 1939 — shows great continuity. The Thai way has evolved through centuries of steadfastness and independence in body and spirit. This has given rise to an unflagging respect for tradition. Nowhere is this more apparent than in the two most vital cohesive forces that are continuous threads running through the national fabric — Buddhism and the monarchy.

Theravada Buddhism was adopted as the national religion during the Sukhothai period and today 94 percent of the population professes and practises the faith. The continuing influence of Buddhism, even in cosmopolitan Bangkok, can be seen in the early morning when files of saffron-robed monks go out into the streets to receive food alms from the lay community. This dawn scene has been the same for hundreds of years.

It is still normal practice for young Thai men to enter the monkhood once in their lives, if only for the usual brief spell of three months. Throughout the country there are an estimated 27,000 Buddhist *wats* (temple-cum-monastery) and at any one time these support roughly 250,000 monks. Far from being a burden to society, this large religious community plays an integral role in the lives of Thais as they engage in the accumulation of merit. The more merit a person gains the closer he or she comes to ultimate release from the cycle of death and rebirth. Giving alms to monks as well as having a son ordained are important ways of gathering merit.

The monarchy also has been a profound influence on the nation since its earliest days. The kings always have directed the country with a firm, but benign, hand. Once known as 'Lords of Life', the kings formerly held absolute power, assumed a semi-divine aura, and enjoyed the highest esteem of their subjects.

Today, following the bloodless revolution of 1932, Thailand is a constitutional monarchy. Curtailment of political power has, however, in no way reduced the king's role to that of a mere figurehead, nor diminished the people's respect.

The present monarch, King Bhumibol Adulyadej, Rama IV, is a man of considerable personal accomplishment as an artist, musician, photographer and yachtsman. He ascended the throne in 1946 at the age of 19 and has subsequently maintained a high and positive profile by taking a hand in initiating and promoting numerous development projects, especially those directed at agricultural improvement. In July 1988 he became the longest reigning monarch in Thai history.

Nearly every home, office, shop and public building throughout the country displays portraits of King Bhumibol and Queen Sirikit, such is the reverence of the Thais for the monarchy and such is its stability and continuity as an institution.

Outside of Bangkok, Thailand still presents a largely rural scene and agriculture, in one form or another, which provides a livelihood for about two-thirds of the population. Although a mainly agrarian society, the country is a dynamic modern economy. In 1985, manufacturing overtook agriculture to account for the largest share of gross national product and today, following an export drive, the world buys not only most of its rice, tapioca and tinned pineapples from Thailand, but also is consuming increasing amounts of the country's shoes, garments, textiles, jewellery, and other manufactured items.

In an economy that has sustained enviable growth over recent years, nothing quite rivals the success of the tourism industry. After a massive promotional campaign in 1987, the country now welcomes 3.5 million visitors a year.

Topographically the country is divided into four distinct areas, each with an individual charm and interest. Stretching north of Bangkok are the Central Plains, a patchwork of emerald green paddies watered by the Chao Phya River, Thailand's Nile. By contrast, the far north is an area of teak forests and jungle-clad mountains, distant and diminutive offshoots of the Himalayas. Here are Doi Inthanon, at 2,565 metres (8,240 feet) the country's highest peak, also a host of small historic towns, forestry work in which elephants are still employed as skilled labour, and the undisturbed villages of colourful hilltribes, people of separate ethnic origin who maintain independent lifestyles little affected by the 20th century.

Different again is the northeast, or I-san in Thai. This is a semi-arid plateau where traditional agricultural communities follow the unchanging annual cycle of farming seasons, punctuated only by many time-honoured festivals. To the south lies the narrow Kra peninsula where the landscape is typified by hilly rain forests and rubber plantations. The coastline, looking out on to the waters of the Andaman Sea on the west and to the Gulf of Thailand on the east, harbours some of Asia's finest beaches and idyllic offshore islands. Most spectacular among the latter are Phuket on the west coast and Samui Island in the Gulf, both offering the beauty of tropical island scenery.

Within Thailand's different landscapes are varied flora and fauna, and much can be appreciated at the several national parks, such as Khao Vai northeast of Bangkok, and others scattered around the country. The forests are dwindling, though lush vegetation still abounds including many types of trees, shrubs and flowers, of which nearly one thousand varieties of orchids are particularly notable. Elephants, tigers, leopards, snakes, monkeys, deer and hundreds of species of birds and butterflies are indigenous to the country.

Despite the beauty of nature, it is Bangkok with its Buddhist temples, unique in form and magnificent in architecture, that is the starting point for most visits. The fabulously ornate yet strangely serene Wat Phra Keo, Temple of the Emerald Buddha, in the compound of the Grand Palace; the imposing *prang* (spire) of Wat Arun, Temple of Dawn, on the banks of the Chao Phya; the extensive compound and giant statue of the reclining Buddha at Wat Po, Bangkok's largest and oldest *wat* — these are just three of the most famous of Bangkok's roughly 400 temples.

Elsewhere in Bangkok cultural achievements also can be seen at the National Museum, one of the best in Asia, and at the private museums of Suan Pakkard Palace and Jim Thompson's house. In both of the latter the houses are as fascinating as the art objects they contain.

Bangkok's environs also are interesting. Up the Chao Phya River there are the ancient ruins of Ayutthaya. To the west lies the world's tallest Buddhist monument, Phra Pathom Chedi, at Nakhom Pathom, and also the infamous Bridge over the River Kwai in Kanchanaburi, built by Allied prisoners of war during World War II.

To the south, for those in search of hedonistic delights, are Phuket and Samui islands, representing the most spectacular and most pristine of Thailand's tropical resorts. An alternative which augments the delights of the beach with on-shore recreation and entertainment is Pattaya resort, only a couple of hours' drive from Bangkok.

Pattaya is unique. It is a beach resort with city status; it is brash, bawdy, colourful and alive with activity. It has a beach which provides a full selection of watersports, but it also offers a profusion of open-air bars, discos, restaurants and other entertainment facilities that produce a nightlife rivalling Bangkok. Bangkok's Pattaya is not to everyone's liking, but it needs to be seen to be believed.

This international playground is on the east coast of the Gulf of Thailand. On the west side, about a three-hour drive from Bangkok, are the more sedate beach resorts of Cha-am and Hua Hin.

Favourite among Thailand's beach resorts is the southern island of Phuket (top) and nearby Phang Nga Bay (above) where fantastically shaped limestone outcrops create an awe-inspiring seascape. Phuket has well-developed tourist facilities and, being roughly the size of Singapore without all the people, affords an opportunity to avoid the madding crowd.

Bangkok at night is a hedonistic city, fun-loving and easy-going. The garish neon lights of go-go bars (top) are a big attraction for some, while youngsters typically flock to huge discotheques, like NASA Spaceadrome (above), which boast the latest high-tech equipment.

Throughout its history, the land now defined by the borders of Thailand has witnessed the passage of a number of civilizations which have been adopted and adapted to varying degrees by the Thais as they forged their sovereign state. Evidence of this cultural evolution abounds, from the pre-Thai period and the various epochs of Thai history. Archaeological finds at the northeastern village of Ban Chiang have yielded evidence of a civilization dating back more than 5,000 years. This pre-dates China and Mesopotamia as the earliest known origins of an agrarian, bronze-making community.

Northeast Thailand also presents some remarkable examples of Khmer architecture, notably at Phimai and Phnom Rung. Dating mostly from the 12th century, these monuments are evidence of the extent of the Khmer empire. Since Angkor, the centre of that empire, is not readily accessible to the ordinary traveller in present-day Kampuchea, the ruins at Phimai and Phnom Rung are the finest examples of Khmer religious architecture that can be seen easily today.

On the northern edge of the Central Plains there is, in addition to Ayutthaya, the site of the first capital at Sukhothai. The extensive ruins here have been the subject of a major UNESCO-backed restoration project and the area has been groomed as an attractive historical park. About 70 kilometres (42 miles) north of Sukhothai are the smaller, but equally fascinating, ruins of Si Satchanalai, a sister city to the first Thai capital.

The major cultural centre outside Bangkok is Chiang Mai, Thailand's second largest city and capital of the North. Chiang Mai was founded in the late 13th century as the capital of Lanna, a Thai kingdom contemporary with, but independent of, Sukhothai. The whole of the North largely was autonomous until the early 20th century and hence displays considerable variation in its art and architecture. The several temples of Chiang Mai, for example, are not only far older than those of Bangkok, they also are vastly different in style and decorative detail.

Today, Chiang Mai extends well beyond the ancient city gates and moat (both of which still can be seen). Besides the fine art, architecture and sculpture of the temples in town and nearby, there is a thriving cottage industry turning out a wide range of traditional handicrafts. Silverware, woodcarving, lacquerware, celadon pottery, and hand-painted umbrellas are produced according to traditional techniques. From Chiang Mai the historic towns Chiang Rai and Chiang Saen, both of which pre-date the founding of Chiang Mai, can be explored. There are also sleepy little settlements, such as Mae Hong Son, hilltribe villages and elephant training camps all hidden away in the timeless folds of the hills.

Scenery and culture are not the sum total of Thailand's attractions. Modern developments, especially in Bangkok, have their own allure. Nightlife entertainment, much of it male-oriented, reaches near legendary proportions. There are also displays of classical Thai dance and music, Thai boxing matches, dinner cruises on the Chao Phya River, concerts, plays, ballet and other classical entertainment. Visiting companies and individual artists of international standing perform in Bangkok from time to time, while a local symphony orchestra and a community theatre group perform regularly. A careful study of the 'What's On' columns in the press shows that Bangkok is not a cultural desert.

There is also food. Thais love food and the national cuisine reflects this passion. Fish and rice are the staples throughout the land, while markets abound in vegetables and fruit, herbs and spices, seafood and farm produce, all of which are imaginatively employed in creative recipes.

Ultimately it is the people who make Thailand what it is. Much is made of Thailand's old soubriquet 'Land of Smiles', but while the Thais are a gentle, hospitable people and more likely to look radiant than to scowl, such a title cheapens the truth with its fairy-tale connotations. There are stresses and strains in Thailand just as in every dynamic society, though what marks the Thais as different is their well-developed sense of fun.

This endearing trait, known as *sanuk*, is visible in nearly every daily activity from a simple stroll to eating, drinking or celebrating. Above all it is given full rein in the numerous festivals that dot the calendar.

Such a delight in the pleasures of life is contagious and is further encouraged by the Thai's inherent graciousness and good manners. The well-known sport of Thai kick-boxing — incidentally the most popular form of spectator *sanuk* — is strangely at odds with this national character in its violent aggression. In daily life the Thais maintain a gentle grace and elegance, which is particularly valuable in a high-powered and fast-paced world.

All this fundamentally derives from the calm and mature desire to integrate traditional and modern values. Essentially it is this that makes the people indelibly Thai and it is this that gives meaning to that famous musical refrain: 'We are Siamese if you please, we are Siamese if you don't please.'

A feature of Bangkok's latter-day development is the mushrooming of glittering department stores and shopping plazas. There is something for everyone among the merchandise — silks, gems and jewellery are among the best buys — while department stores themselves are popular places for the Thai pastime of pai teeo, *going for a stroll simply to see and be seen.*

Bangkok is notorious for its traffic jams, lines of halted cars, buses and trucks, with motorcycles, often carrying entire families, buzzing in between. Such congestion can be frustrating but there is no solution and the visitor should learn the wisdom of the common Thai expression mai pen rai, 'never mind, it doesn't matter'.

Following page
The Chao Phya River was originally Bangkok's focal point and major highway, but 20th-century development led inevitably away from its banks. Today it is back in vogue as a number of modern deluxe hotels, like the Royal Orchid Sheraton (top), have opted for river frontage to become neighbours of the famous Oriental Hotel (centre).

Classical Thai architecture, as seen in
temples and palaces, such as the Dusit
Maha Prasad Hall of Bangkok's Grand
Palace (above) is the very image of Oriental
wonder. The exteriors are highly ornate and
characterized by multi-tiered roofs, while
interior decoration is no less inspired, as
seen in this mid-19th century mural at Wat
Rajapradit (right).

Two Kinnari *(left)* dance on the surface of a lacquer cabinet now in the Bangkok National Library. In Thai tradition *Kinnari* are mythical beings with the head and torso of a woman and the wings and legs of a bird which inhabit the legendary Himalayan forests. The cabinet is from Thailand's former capital, Ayutthaya. Other figures from myth and Buddhist belief are depicted on a typical temple doorway *(right)*.

At Wat Arun (top), gilded Buddhas are haloed by a richly painted mural of flowers, leaves and birds. On the roof of the royal Palace (right), sunlight glints on a gold and red statue of Garuda, the mythical winged mount of the Hindu god Vishnu. At Chiang Mai's Wat Pha Pong (above left), animals and birds are depicted in lively and detailed carvings by traditional craftsmen.

The Thais excel in the decorative arts and this is nowhere more apparent than in the kaleidoscopic sight of Bangkok's dazzling Wat Phra Keo, Temple of the Emerald Buddha (opposite).

Thais are devout Buddhists and 94 percent of the population professes and practises the religion. Adherence to the faith is readily witnessed in the richness of the country's temples (left). However, Buddhism is an accommodating religion and the people may also seek blessing and good fortune at other auspicious shrines, like Bangkok's Erawan Shrine (above) which honours the Hindu god Brahma and is widely believed to grant wishes.

Wat Arun (left) and other historic temples stand as silent witnesses to Thailand's cultural heritage, but they have not been reduced to mere hollow monuments. The nature of Buddhism in Thailand imbues all shrines with an air of serenity and deep reverence. Orange-robed monks (right) remain an integral part of the daily scene at temples all over the country.

Saffron-robed monks, most from the Theravada school of Buddhism, are a daily sight throughout Thailand. Early in the morning monks walk through the streets to receive food alms from the people, continuing a tradition dating back centuries. Such giving is an opportunity for ordinary people to 'make merit'.

31

The classical mode in Thai art and architecture has not remained static and has received fresh stylistic input at various times. Wat Benchamabopit (above), the Marble Temple built by King Chulalongkorn, is a superb example of developing religious architecture at the turn of the century. In the modern age, a classical-style painting (left) by a leading contemporary artist, Panya Vijinthanasarn, adorns the Thai pavilion at Expo 88 in Brisbane, Australia.

Farmers at work in the paddy fields (left) and labourers dusted with tapioca flour (above) are typical images of Thailand's agriculture; the country is the world's fifth largest food exporter, with rice and tapioca topping a list of varied produce. Despite the importance of agriculture, farming is still largely unmechanised and adheres to traditional ways and techniques.

Ancient monuments from various phases of history attest to past glories. Phnom Rung (left), a 12th-century Khmer temple in the Northeast, is a fine example of the artistic achievement of the Khmer empire centred on Angkor. The ruins of Ayutthaya (top), the Thai capital for more than 400 years until destroyed by the Burmese in 1767, and art treasures preserved in the local museum (above) bear witness to what was once the most magnificent city in Southeast Asia.

The Thai nation was founded at Sukhothai, on the northern edge of the Central Plains, in the early 13th century. The ruins of the ancient capital are today preserved in an historic park, site of the most impressive celebration of Loy Krathong, a national festival believed to be have originated there. Held in honour of the 'Mother of Waters' on the night of the full moon in November, it is a festival of lights in which krathongs, lotus-shaped offerings, are floated on the ponds.

Following page
At the centre of Sukhothai stand the ruins of Wat Mahathat, dominated by a statue of the seated Buddha. It was here that Theravada Buddhism was first adopted as the national religion and where Thai arts first flowered. Indeed, the religious, cultural and social roots of the Thai can all be traced back to Sukhothai, which means 'Dawn of Happiness'.

The north and northeast regions of the country offer some magnificent natural scenery as the monotony of the Central Plains gives way to the splendour of mountains, hidden valleys, rivers and waterfalls. Scenes vary from the picturesque (above) to breathtaking vistas of mist-shrouded peaks (left) at Phu Kraduang in Loei Province.

Thai women are renowned for their good looks and natural charm. This becomes readily apparent at any of the numerous upcountry fairs and festivals, like the Flower Festival held in Chiang Mai in February. Central to these lively, colourful affairs are parades of decorative floats and beauty pageants. Whatever the occasion — they generally celebrate some bounty of the land — a 'Miss Chiang Mai' or 'Miss Lamyai' or whomever will be selected from a bevy of local beauties.

Chiang Mai, the main city of northern Thailand, is arguably the world's largest centre for cottage industries. Here numerous traditional handicrafts survive as skills have been handed down from generation to generation. At the little village of Bor Sand, just outside Chiang Mai, handmade umbrellas are the local speciality. Crafted from handmade paper stretched over a split bamboo frame, the shades are covered with delightful designs applied with uncanny ease by skilled artists.

Handmade dolls, either as single figures or in tableaux (above), capture in miniature the expressive postures and magnificent costumes of the classical masked khon dance drama. The detail is superb and the masks of the various demon characters (right) are fashioned as separate, detachable pieces.

Following page
Northern Thai temple murals, as seen in this detail from Wat Phra Singh, Chiang Mai are fascinating for their depictions of local dress and customs. They are characterized by a certain joie de vivre and a love of homely detail that make them less intellectual and more sensual than their counterparts in Bangkok.

48

Wat Phra Singh, like other temples in Chiang Mai and the North, presents a style of architecture unique to the region. Most notably the multi-tiered roofs are more pronounced with their sweeping low eaves, and the facades are masterpieces of the woodcarver's art.

Flower covered hillsides and hilltribe folk in distinctive tribal costumes are typical sights in northern Thailand. As well as being different in its landscape, the North presents a contrast to other parts of the country; its culture has largely evolved through separate development. The region once formed the independent Thai kingdom of Lanna and it was not until the early 20th century that the area came fully under the control of the central government in Bangkok.

Silver is the traditional symbol of wealth among the hilltribes of northern Thailand. The metal was originally obtained in the form of coins from British India or French Indochina, though today it is imported in ingots via Bangkok. Silversmiths fashion a huge array of jewellery: bracelets, headpieces, earrings and splendid necklaces with intricately crafted numerous pendants. Many of the most spectacular pieces are part of traditional wedding costumes.

Northern Thailand is home to seven principal hilltribe minorities, people of separate ethnic origin who follow independent lifestyles, to a large degree unaffected by the 20th century. This Akha girl (left) still sports the colourful finery of her tribal costume, as do most hilltribe women, but the advances of mainstream society are no longer totally absent. Various government welfare programmes are operated, including education for hilltribe children (above).

Whether young Akha girls in their traditional silver-ornamented head-dresses (above) or a pipe-smoking Karen grandmother (right), hilltribe women continue to present a picture of enduring customs and lifestyles. The men, however, have today mostly abandoned the attire traditional to their tribe, and they dress like any other Thai farmer. Nevertheless, a visit to a hilltribe village still affords a glimpse into a unique world.

Yao women and children with their typically bright red boa collars and pom poms add a splash of colour in the landscape of the northern hills. Villages of thatched huts are scattered throughout the mist-shrouded mountains and are popular destinations for trekking expeditions.

A hilltribe baby casts a curious eye at the camera. As tourism develops in the North, the ethnic minorities are becoming more and more used to exposure to the outside world. It is a mixed blessing; while it can bring advantages in social welfare, it also changes values.

Following page
Idyllic Surat Thani Beach on Koh Samui.

Both east and west coastlines of Thailand's southern peninsula offer superb choices of beaches and offshore islands. There are spots that look as deserted and as inviting as Robinson Crusoe's refuge (left) and areas which have become major attractions, such as the so-called 'James Bond Island' (above) in Phang Nga Bay, location for the movie 'The Man With the Golden Gun'.

Of all Thailand's beach resort destinations none are quite so spectacular as Phuket Island and the more secluded nearby Phi Phi Islands (above). Warm turquoise seas, an azure sky, beaches of powdery white sand and tropical vegetation in vivid greens make for a spell-binding combination. It all seems wonderfully removed from today's world, though Phuket is just an hour's flight from Bangkok.

Following page
Sunset at Phang Nga Bay in southern Thailand. Prehistoric rock paintings have been found in this region and, with its curiously shaped limestone outcrops and mangrove swamps along the shore, the setting at this tranquil moment gives rise to a sense of the primeval.

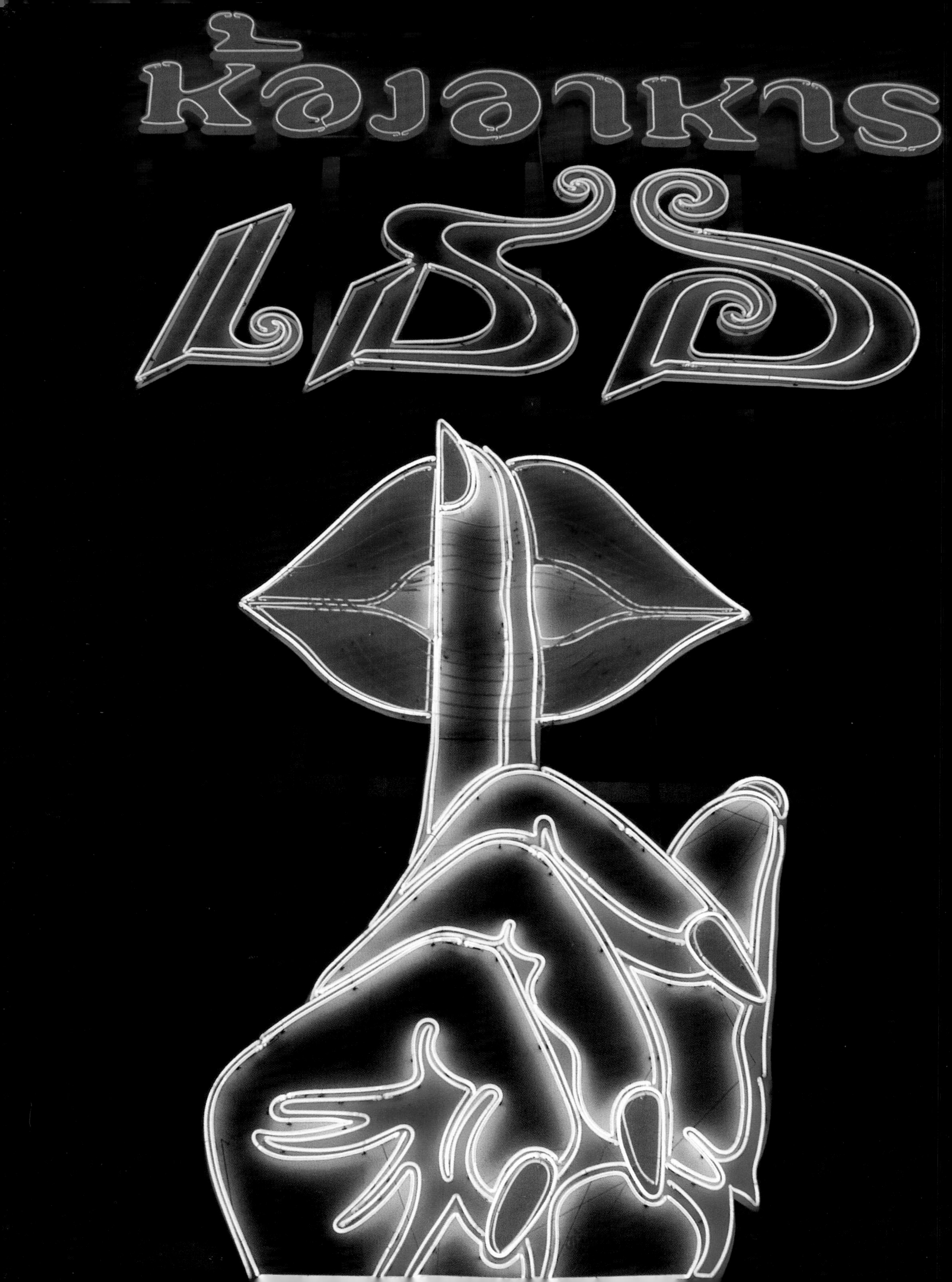
ห้องอาหาร

Go-go bars (above and left) are the most famous of Bangkok's nightlife attractions. Scantily-clad girls dance to the beat in a scene that is surprisingly easy-going and happily lacking in that sense of pathos found in similar places in the West. A neon sign (far left) looks like a symbol of Bangkok nightlife, though it simply advertises a restaurant.

Female impersonator shows (left) are popular in Bangkok and the beach resort of Pattaya, though it is the neon lights of Patpong Road (above and right), centre of Bangkok's go-go bar district, that attract the single male.

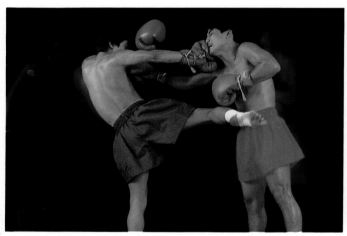

The Thai propensity for sanuk, *fun, or having a good time, finds expression in many ways. Most popular among spectator sports is Thai kick boxing (above) in which feet, knees and elbows are brought into play as well as gloved fists. For such a gentle people as the Thais, it is a strangely aggressive sport. In a lighter vein, this man (right) makes a living from wrestling crocodiles at the Crocodile Farm, a well-known tourist attraction on the outskirts of Bangkok.*

Following page
Sunset at Koh Samui presents an idyllic picture. Located in the Gulf of Thailand, off the southern coast, the island is characterized by splendid, uncluttered beaches and a lush green hinterland. Cultivating coconut groves and fishing are the principal occupations among the local inhabitants.

AN A TO Z OF FUN FACTS

A

Air Travel Over 50 international airlines serve Bangkok's Don Muang airport.

Ayuddhaya Until it was sacked by a marauding Burmese army in 1767, Ayuddhaya was Siam's capital city for almost 300 years. Early foreign traders described it as one of the most spectacular cities on earth during its height in the 17th and 18th centuries.

B

Ban Chiang A small village in Northeast Thailand, Ban Chiang was put on the archaeologist's map in the 1970s when a remarkable find of pottery and bronze tools established the fact that an advanced civilization existed in this region as long ago as 5000 BC, predating the earliest bronze finds from anywhere else in the world.

Bangkok Thailand's capital city of some eight million people is the fastest growing major city in the world today. It bursts under an inadequate infrastructure and many visitors find the traffic and heat (it is rated as the hottest metropolitan area in the world) hard to take. But those who do take the time to explore are rewarded by its many virtues.

Bridge over the River Kwai An infamous bridge constructed by prisoners of war interned in Thailand during the Second World War. The railway bridge was needed to complete a Thailand–Burma rail link so the Japanese could move material over the rugged terrain which separates the two countries. 36,000 prisoners of war lost their lives in this effort. The bridge was eventually destroyed by Allied aerial bombing.

C

Chai Dee A Thai phrase which literally translates as 'good heart'. For the Thais this is the ultimate compliment since it means generosity, kindliness, humility and purity of spirit and mind.

Chiang Mai Thailand's largest city in the North and the former capital of the ancient Lanna Kingdom. Established in 1255 by King Mengrai.

Climate Thailand lies entirely within the tropics and thus never experiences any cold weather to speak of. There are three seasons; the rainy season from May to October, the warm and dry season of November to February, and the hot and dry season of March to mid-May. The warm and dry season is the best time to visit Thailand and the hot and dry season is the worst.

Crocodiles Crocodiles were once so prevalent in the rivers of Thailand that they posed a serious hazard. Now they exist almost solely on 'farms' which cultivate them for the export of their skins and other by-products. The Bangkok crocodile farm boasts having in captivity the world's largest crocodile, a 30-year old monster that has grown to some 10 m (33 ft) long.

D

Deforestation Almost 75% of Thailand's original forest cover has been eliminated in the past 30 years. A total ban on all logging in the country has finally been instigated.

Doi Suthep The mountain which overlooks Chiang Mai and cradles one of Thailand's most famous temples, Wat Prathat, as well as the royal summer residence, Bhuping Palace

E

Economy The economy of Thailand is based in equal parts on agriculture, (rice cultivation still employs 65% of the working population), and manufacturing which is the most rapidly expanding sector of the economy. In 1989 Thailand enjoyed the largest growth in real GNP in the world (11–12%) and is soon to join the ranks of the 'newly industrialized nations' for better or for worse. Tourism is the single largest earner of foreign exchange with over five million visitors from overseas in 1989.

Elephants The elephant has a special place in the history of Thailand and in the people's hearts. Domesticated for a millennia for work and warfare, the elephant was even featured on the original Siamese flag. White (actually albino) elephants have been especially treasured and any found must be turned over to the King. There are still 2–3,000 wild elephants inhabiting the forests of Thailand.

Emerald Buddha Actually composed of green jasper, the Emerald Buddha is the spiritual symbol of Thailand. Its origin is a mystery but it can be traced back to Laos in the 12th century, since when it has graced the central temple of every successive Thai capital. Currently it is housed in a special viharn in the Wat Pra Keo temple in Bangkok.

Ethnic groups Immigrant Chinese make up the largest ethnic minority in Thailand (perhaps about 10% of the total population). They have become assimilated to such a great extent, however, that it is often difficult to tell who is really Chinese and who isn't. A dozen different hilltribes living in the mountains of northern Thailand total about 700,000 and comprise the most colourful element of the nation's minorities.

F

Food Food is abundant in this verdant land, indeed Thailand is one of only six nations in the world that exports more food than it imports. The Thai people are natural gourmets producing one of the worlds greatest cuisines and eating almost incessantly! Bangkok boasts more than 10,000 eating establishments including the ubiquitous street vendor.

Fruits Perhaps the most delicious and exotic of all Thailand's fruits is the mangosteen, a hard, round, purple fruit the size of a pool ball inside which are soft, white, juicy sections. Queen Victoria once offered 100 pounds sterling to anyone who could bring her one; they don't travel well — spoiling in just a few days even with refrigeration.

G

Golden Triangle The infamous 'Golden Triangle' comprises the hills of northern Thailand, the Shan State of Burma and the western region of Laos where opium is cultivated and processed into heroin in jungle laboratories. This region is responsible for up to 60% of the world's illicit heroin supply.

H

Highest point The highest mountain in the country is Doi Inthanon, rising in northern Thailand to an altitude of 2,590 metres (8,514 feet).

I

Indian Influences In many ways Thailand is as much a Hindu culture as a Buddhist one. The Thai language has its origin in Sanskrit, and all royal ceremonies are performed by Brahmin priests, not Buddhists. Many of the popular animistic beliefs are Indian in origin as well.

K

The King Thailand's ruling monarch since 1946, King Bhumipol is a true renaissance man. A poet, musician (he played with Benny Goodman at one time!), scientist and man of the people, the King represents the epitome of the benevolent monarch.

Koh Samui An island off the southern coast in the Gulf of Thailand which, once a haven for budget travellers, now attracts up-scale tourists as well, especially since an airport was opened in 1989.

L

Loy Kratong Celebrated on the night of the full moon of November, Loy Kratong is Thailand's loveliest holiday event. An animist celebration commemorating the female spirit of the waters. People build small candle-lit floats and send them adrift on the nation's waterways.

M

Mai Pen Rai A Thai expression which translated literally means 'never mind'. In many ways this phrase represents the easy-going attitude towards life that makes the people of the country so endearing to outsiders. On the other hand it also represents a facet of Thai culture that foreign businessmen can find incredibly frustrating.

O

Orchids There are over 1,000 species of orchids in Thailand and their cultivation and export is a major industry. Some of the wild species are extremely rare, like the Blue Vanda (*Vanda cerulea*) which is unique to Thailand and worth over US$1,000 for a single specimen.

P

Phang-nga Bay Perhaps one of the most interesting landscapes to be found anywhere in Thailand are the limestone islands of Phang-nga Bay just north of Phuket Island in southern Thailand. Needle-like rocks jut up to 500 m (1,600 ft) above the ocean's surface.

Phuket Until it was discovered for tourism, the islanders of Phuket enjoyed prosperity as a result of tin mining and rubber trees. The beaches on the island's west coast were inaccessible from the mining areas because of a range of mountains. Consequently nobody thought twice about these beaches and the few fisherman who lived there were considered hermit eccentrics. Now, many of those fishermen are wealthier than the tin mine owners for Phuket is Thailand's foremost beach resort.

Population Thailand's population is 58,000,000 — about the same as that of France or West Germany. Bangkok has around 8,000,000 making it the largest city beween Calcutta and Shanghai.

Q

The Queen Thailand's beautiful Queen Sirikit met King Bhumipol when he was studying in Switzerland in 1948. The King had been in a car accident in which he lost his right eye. Sirikit was the daughter of a Thai diplomat based in London and visited Bhumipol in the hospital while he was recuperating. They were married shortly thereafter.

R

Railways Thailand has an excellent rail network linking the northeast, north and south to Bangkok. The southern line runs all the way to Singapore and is a three-day, two-night journey. The best way to travel is by second class reserved sleeper, only about US$15 to Chiang Mai or US$40 to Singapore.

Religions Some 95% of the Thai population are Buddhists, 4% are Muslim who live in the southern provinces bordering Malaysia, and the remaining 1% are hilltribe animists or Christians.

S

Sawasdee *Sawasdee* is the Thai word of greeting, whether you are coming or going. Men say *Sawasdee Krap* and women say *Sawasdee Kha*, usually accompanied by a *wai* — the traditional form of addressing someone with the palms pressed together, fingers pointing upwards and hands held just below chin level.

Siam Until the Second World War Thailand was known as Siam. The name was changed to Thailand because a highly nationalistic government came to power under the fascist Pibul Songkram regime and Thailand, meaning 'land of the free' was meant to arouse the population's patriotic spirit. After the war and Pibul's disgrace (he backed the Japanese) the name was changed back to Siam, but for some reason 'Thailand' was reinstated again after several months.

Siamese Cats There is a breed of cat unique to Thailand but it is not the one we commonly call 'Siamese'. The true Siamese cat has very short gray hair covering the entire body and a few black highlights on the tip of the nose and other facial extremities. This cat also has large ears and occasionally blue eyes. They are very rare as pure breeds, costing at least $500 in Thailand if you can find one. The common Siamese cat, which we are all aware of, is a breed that was bred originally from the real Siamese but has been diluted considerably over time by cat enthusiasts.

T

Jim Thompson A Second World War American intelligence officer who stayed on in Thailand after the war ended, Jim Thompson revived the Thai silk industry and developed one of the finest classical Thai art collections in private hands. His disappearance one afternoon in 1968 while taking a walk in Malaysia's Cameron Highlands remains one of the great mysteries of modern times.

U

Utapao airbase The largest of USA bases in Thailand during the Vietnam War was Utapao, located near Pattaya. At the peak of the war it was the 'busiest' airport in the world. There were 50,000 US servicemen stationed in Thailand by 1970, and Bangkok was one of the rest-and-recreation locations offered to weary GIs.

V

Visa requirements Westerners do not need a visa for visits less than 15 days. Tourist visas, good for two months with a one-month extension possible, may be obtained from any Thai consulate abroad. If you stay for a total of more than 90 days during any one calendar year a tax clearance certificate must be obtained from the Labour Department in Bangkok.

W

Wat A *wat* is a Thai temple and the architectural symbol of Thailand. There are literally thousands of wats in Thailand dotting the landscape in every corner of the Kingdom.

Z

Zoos Bangkok's Dusit Zoo is a good place to while away an afternoon and escape from the city's heat and confusion. Chiang Mai also has a zoo located at the base of Doi Suthep. The zoo began as a shelter for wild animals brought down from the hills by hilltribesmen and hunters and confiscated by the Thai Border Patrol.

INDEX